CALCULATING COMPANION

FOR

THE SLIDE RULE

CONTAINING

Instructions for its Application

TO

CALCULATIONS OF LEVERAGE, MENSURATION OF SUPERFICES,
SOLIDS, &c., CASK AND MALT GAUGING, STEAM
ENGINES, METAL WEIGHING, &c.

BY JAMES L. ROWLAND.

LONDON:
WALTON AND MABERLY,
UPPER GOWER STREET, AND IVY LANE, PATERNOSTER ROW.
—
1855.

[Entered at Stationers' Hall.]

INTRODUCTION.

———

It is hoped that the accompanying little book will meet with the general approbation of the public; more particularly as it contains instructions on several subjects connected with the Slide Rule, which have not appeared in any other book, and which have been discovered by the Author, after a good deal of thought and application.

It is published in the hope that calculations will thereby be facilitated; and those to whom "time is money," will find themselves amply repaid by the purchase of this unpretending little work.

CONTENTS.

CALCULATING COMPANION,

ETC. ETC.

INSTRUCTIONS FOR USING THE SLIDE RULE.

On the rule there are four lines of numbers, called A, B, C, D; the upper three of which are exactly alike, consisting of two radiuses numbered from left hand to right hand, 1, 2, 3, 4, 5, 6, 7, 8, 9 — 1, 2, 3, 4, 5, 6, 7, 8, 9, 10; these three are, generally speaking, used for superficial measure. The lowest, or girt line D, differs from the others, as its first number is 4, and last 40. All questions in solid or cubic measure are answered on this, whether timber, stone, bricks, earth, metal, gauging, &c., by setting figures on the sliding part of the rule to different gauge points on this.

NUMERATION

Is the first thing which ought to be learnt in regard to this rule. It is a very simple subject, and when it is known everything else is easily understood. The numbers and divisions are all arbitrary, and the value set upon them must be such as the nature of the question requires; as, whatever you call the first 1, the middle 1 must be increased tenfold, and the end 1, of course, in another tenfold proportion.

A 2

Example 1. Let it be required to find 16 on the top line, or line A; look for the first or middle 1 (it matters not which), and count six of the long divisions between that and 2, which will be 16, the number for which we are seeking; it is also 160, 1600, 16000, &c.

Ex. 2. Let the number 4825 be required; find a 4 on the top line and consider it 4000; then count eight of the divisions between that and 5, which is 800, and a quarter of the distance between the eighth and ninth division is 25. This is also 482·5, 48·25, 4·825, &c.

MULTIPLICATION.

RULE.—Set the multiplier on B to 1 or 10 on A, and opposite any multiplicand upon A is the product on B.

Ex. 1. What is the product of 9 times 6? Set 9 upon B to 1 on A, and against 6 on A is 54—the answer on B.

Ex. 2. What is the product of 74 times 16? Set 74 upon B to 1 on A, and opposite 16 on A is 1184 on B.

Where the answer amounts to four figures or more, as in the last example, it is not easy to distinguish the unit numbers on the rule; it is, therefore, found to be a great assistance to multiply the unit numbers mentally, and as 4 times 6 is 24, the last or unit number must be 4.

DIVISION.

As the divisor on B is to 1 or 10 upon A, so is the dividend on B to the quotient on A.

Ex. Divide £96 between 8 persons. Set 8 upon B to 1 or 10 on A, and against 96 on B is 12 upon A.

RULE OF THREE.

In this rule we have three numbers given to find a fourth, that shall bear the same proportion to the third as the second does to the first. The slide should be set in this manner :—As the first term upon A is to the second on B, so is the third term on A to the fourth upon B; always remembering to take the first and third terms on the same line, and the second and fourth on the other.

Ex. 1. If a man can walk 16 miles in 4 hours, how long would he require to walk 100 miles? Set 16 upon B to 4 on A, and opposite 100 on B is 25 upon A.

Ex. 2. If 7 cwts. cost 27s. 6d., what will 9 tons cost? Set 7 upon B to 27·5 on A, and opposite 9 on B is £35 7s. 1¾d. upon A. When any number of cwts. is thus set on B to its value on A, it is a table of tons in weight, and pounds in money; for against any other number of tons upon B is the price in pounds and parts of a pound on A.

When more requires less, or less requires more, the slide must be inverted, as :—If 15 men do a piece of work in 9 days, how many can do it in 5 days? Set 9 on C to 15 upon A, and against 5 on C is 27, the answer, on A.

If I lend my friend £200 for 12 months, for how long ought he to lend me £150? Set 200 on C to 12 upon A, opposite 150 on C is 16 on A.

LEVERAGE.

Questions with regard to leverage can be answered on this rule with great ease, always observing that the slide should be inverted.

CASE I.—Knowing the length of lever, the power of force, and distance between weight and fulcrum, to ascertain what weight can be lifted :—Set amount of power on C to distance from fulcrum to power upon A ; opposite the distance from weight to fulcrum on A is the weight that can be lifted on C.

Ex. If I have a lever 88 inches in length, power of force equal to 94 lbs. at one end, and fulcrum 9 inches from weight, how many pounds can I lift ? Set 94 on C to 79 upon A, opposite 9 on A is 825 lbs. on C.

CASE II.—Other particulars being known, except at what distance the fulcrum is to be placed from the weight, set amount of force on C to total length in inches of lever upon A; opposite the weight to be lifted is the distance at which the fulcrum must be placed.

Ex. At what distance must I place the fulcrum from weight of 23 cwts., having power of 54 lbs., and lever 12 feet in length ? Set 54 on C to 144 upon A, opposite 2576 (number of lbs.) on C is 3 inches full.

CASE III.—To ascertain the power required :— Set distance from weight to fulcrum on C to weight to be lifted on A, opposite distance from fulcrum to power on C is power required on A.

Ex. What power will be required to lift 170 lbs., with a lever 94 inches long, and fulcrum 7 inches from weight? Set 7 on C to 170 on A, opposite 87 upon C is 13·7 lbs. on A.

CASE IV.—To discover at what distance from weight the power ought to be applied. Set rule in same manner as CASE III., only look for reply on C, opposite amount of power upon A.

Having power equal to 22 lbs., and wishing to lift 214 lbs. with fulcrum 4 inches from weight, what must be the distance to apply that power? Set 4 on C to 214 upon A, opposite 22 on A is 39 bare on C.

POWER BETWEEN THE FULCRUM AND WEIGHT.

I. To ascertain at what distance from the fulcrum power must be applied :—Set length of lever upon C to weight on A, opposite power on C is distance upon A.

Ex. With a lever 120 inches long, and 54 lbs. weight at one end, at what distance from the fulcrum must 216 lbs. be applied? Set 120 on C to 54 upon A; opposite 216 on C is 30 inches upon A.

II. To ascertain what weight can be lifted. Set amount of power upon C to the distance the weight is from fulcrum on A, and opposite length of lever on C is weight upon A.

Ex. With a lever 92 inches long, amount of force equal to 136 lbs., what weight can be lifted 8 inches from fulcrum? Set 136 on C to 8 upon A; against 92 on C is 11·8 lbs. upon A.

III. To ascertain what amount of strength is required :—Set length of lever on C to weight to be lifted upon A; opposite distance from fulcrum to weight on A is answer upon C.

IV. To ascertain the length the lever must be :—

Set amount of force on C to distance from fulcrum to force upon A, and opposite the weight to be lifted on C is length of lever upon A.

VULGAR AND DECIMAL FRACTIONS.

I. In reducing a fraction to its equivalent decimal, set 1 upon B to the denominator on A, then opposite the numerator on A is the required decimal upon B.

Ex. Reduce ₁₄⁄₃₇ to its decimal. Set 1 on B to 37 upon A; opposite 14 on A is ·3783 upon B.

II. To find a multiplier to a divisor that shall perform the same by multiplication as the divisor would by division. Set the divisor upon A to 1 on B; opposite 1 on A is the required number upon B.

Ex. What will be the multiplier to 75? Set 1 on B to 75 upon A; opposite 1 on A is ·1333 + on B.

III. Knowing multiplier to find a divisor:—Set 1 upon B to the multiplier on A; opposite 1 on A is the divisor on B.

Ex. What is the divisor for .04? Set 1 upon B to ·04 on A, and against 1 upon A is ·25 on B.

IV. To reduce lower denominations to decimal fractions of higher denominations:—Set the number of the given article in that to which you wish to reduce it on B to 1 upon A; opposite your given number on A is the required decimal.

Ex. 1. Reduce 4s. 8d. to its decimal of a pound. As there are 240 pence in a pound, set 1 on B to 240 upon A; opposite 56 on A is ·2343 on B.

Ex. 2. Reduce 1 foot 7 inches to its decimal of

a yard. Set 1 on B to 36 upon A; opposite 19 on A is ·528 on B.

Ex. 3. What decimal of an acre is 3 roods 8 poles of land? As there are 160 poles in an acre, set 1 upon B to 160 on A; opposite 128 on A is ·8 upon B.

Ex. 4. Reduce 14 cwt. 1 qr. to its decimal of a ton. Set 1 on B to 80 upon A (the number of qrs. in a ton); opposite 57 on A is ·7125 on B.

V. To find the value of a decimal fraction, set 1 on B to the given decimal upon A, and opposite the number of that to which you wish to reduce it, to make one whole number on B, is its number upon A.

Ex. 1. How many pence are contained in ·2343 of £1? Set 1 on B to 2343 upon A, and opposite 240 on B is 56 on A.

Ex. 2. What number of inches are contained in ·528 of a yard? Set 1 on B to 528 upon A; opposite 36 on B is 19 inches upon A.

Ex. 3. How many poles in ·8 of an acre? Set 1 upon B to 8 upon A; against 160 on B is 128 on A.

Ex. 4. How many quarters in ·7125 of a ton? Set 1 on B to 7125 upon A; opposite 80 on B is 57 upon A. Or if you wish to ascertain the number of pounds, opposite 2240 upon B is 1596 on A.

SQUARE ROOT.

MEAN PROPORTION, ETC.

To extract the square root of any number, set 10 upon C to 10 upon D, and opposite any number upon C is its root on D; thus, opposite squares 16, 25, 36 on C are roots 4, 5, 6, &c., on D; and in the same manner squares and roots of all numbers may be found.

To find a mean or geometrical proportion between two numbers, set one of them upon C to the same number on D, and opposite the other upon C is the mean number on D.

Ex. 1. What is the mean proportion between 70 and 96? Set 96 on C to 96 upon D, and opposite 70 on C is 82 upon D, which is the mean number sought.

Ex. 2. Find the mean proportion between 7 and 175? Set 175 upon C to same number on D; against 7 on C is 35 upon D.

Ex. 3. The wall of a castle is 45 feet high, and surrounded with a ditch 60 feet broad; what length must a ladder be to reach from the outside of the ditch to the top of the castle? After squaring the height of the tower, and the breadth of the ditch, add them together, and extract square root of the sum, which will give the length of the ladder; for opposite to 5625 upon C is 75 on D.

Ex. 4. Two ships sail from the same port at the same time, both going about equal speed; one of them goes due east 50 leagues, the other due south; how far are they then distant? The square of 50 being 2500, that multiplied by 2, as both ships are at the same distance from starting place, we find against 5000 on C 70·79 leagues upon D.

CUBE ROOT, &c.

The cube of any number may be found by setting the number on C to 10 on D; opposite that number upon D is its cube on C.

Ex. What is the cube of 5 ? Set 5 on C to 10 upon D, and against that number 5 on D is **125** upon C.

To extract the cube root, the slide must be inverted ; then put the given number on B to 10 upon D, and where the figures exactly coincide on those lines is the root required.

Ex. 1. What is the cube root of 27 ? Set 27 on B to 10 upon D, and against 3 on D is 3 upon B, which is the required root.

Ex. 2. What is the cube root of 512 ? Set that number upon B to 10 on D, and you will then find that the figure 8 coincides on those two lines.

Ex. 3. If the solid contents of a globe be **10648,** what will be the length of the side of a cube of equal solidity ? Set given number on B to same upon D, and 22 is the number which is found to have, on both those lines, an agreement.

MENSURATION OF SUPERFICES,

AS BOARDS, WAINSCOTING, PAVING, PLASTERING, SLATING, PAINTING, GLAZING, LAND SURVEYING, ETC.

When all dimensions are in feet, set length on B to 10 on A, and opposite width upon A is superficial contents on B. With length in feet, and breadth in inches, set length upon B to 12 on A ; but if all dimensions are inches, let 144 be the gauge point.

Ex. 1. How many superficial feet are there in a board 18 feet long and 17 inches wide ? Set 18 upon B to 12 on A, and against 17 on A is 25½ feet on B.

Ex. 2. In a door 7½ feet high and 3½ feet wide, how many superficial feet are there ? Set 75 on B to 10 upon A, and opposite 3·5 on A is 26·25 feet upon B.

B

Ex. 3. What number of superficial feet will a window 60 inches in height, and 45 in width, contain? Set 60 on B to 144 upon A, then against 45 on A is 18 feet 9 inches upon B.

PAINTING

is, generally speaking, measured by the square yard, equal to 9 superficial feet; this is done on the same plan as other measuring, only the length upon B must be set to 9 on A, and opposite the height or breadth in feet on A will be the answer in superficial yards on B.

Ex. How much painting have we in a piece, 47 feet in length, and 17 feet in width? Set 47 upon B to 9 on A, and against 17 on A is 88 yards 7 feet upon B.

PAPER HANGING.

When the dimensions of a room about to be papered are known, and you wish to ascertain how many pieces it will require, set 63 (the number of superficial feet in a piece) on B to the entire distance round the room upon A, and opposite to the height of the room on B is the number of pieces required upon A.

Ex. How many pieces of paper shall we want for a room 24 feet long, 16 feet wide, 9½ feet high? After ascertaining circumference of room by saying $24 + 16 \times 2 = 80$, set 63 upon B to 80 on A, and opposite 9½ on B is fully 12 pieces upon A.

SLATING.

After having ascertained the number of superficial feet which require covering with slates, set 1 upon

B to the gauge points below on A, and against the number of superficial feet on B will be upon A the number of slates required :—

	2-in. lap.	2¼-in. lap.	3-in. lap.
Duchess	109	112	114
Vis-duchess	120	123	126
Countess..........	160	165	170
Vis-countess	180	186	193
Ladies............	258	265	275

Ex. 1. If we have a roof to be covered with countess slates, having the 2¼-in. lap, 43 feet × 25 feet, how many will be required ? By setting 43 upon B to 1 on A, we see against 25 upon A, the roof contains 1075 feet; then set 1 upon B to 165 on A, and opposite 1075 on B is 1773 upon A.

Ex. 2. How many duchess slates will be required for a roof of the same size, and having the same lap? Set 1 on B to 112 upon A, and against 1075 on B is 1204 upon A.

For plain tiles multiply the superficial contents of roof in squares by 600; and for pantiles by 120.

LAND MEASURING.

The gauge points for measuring land are the number of square chains, perches, or yards contained in an acre. If the dimensions are in chains, the gauge point is 10; if in perches, 160; and if in yards, 4840 on A; to which the length upon B must be set, and opposite the breadth upon A will be the superficial contents in acres on B.

Ex. 1. How many acres are there in a field 30 chains 50 links long, and 5 chains 60 links broad? Set 30·5 upon B to 1 on A, and against 5·6 upon A are 170 acres on B,

Ex. 2. What are the contents of a field 43·15 perches long and 17·5 perches wide? Set 43·15 upon B to 160 on A; against 17·5 upon A are 4·72 acres on B.

Ex. 3. How many acres are there in a piece of land 536 yards long and 280 yards wide? Set 536 on B to 4840 upon A, and against 280 on A are 31 acres upon B.

TO ASCERTAIN THE CONVEX SURFACE OF A GLOBE.

Set 8 upon C to 16 on D, and opposite the diameter of the globe on D is the number of superficial inches, feet, yards, &c., upon C.

Ex. What is the superficial measure of a globe the diameter of which is 9 inches? Set 8 upon C to 16 on D, and against 9 on D is 254 inches upon C.

OF A CIRCLE.

I. Knowing the diameter, to ascertain the circumference; or, knowing the circumference, to find the diameter :—Set 7 on B to 22 upon A, and opposite any diameter upon B is its circumference on A.

II. To find the length of side of the greatest square that can be inscribed in any given circle :—Set 6 upon B to 8·5 on A, and against the diameter of the circle upon A is the length of side of inscribed square on B.

III. To ascertain the length of side of a square equal in area to any given circle :—Set 8 upon B to 9 on A, then opposite any diameter of a circle on A is the length of side of square equal to it on B, and *vice versâ*.

IV. Knowing diameter to ascertain area, or area to find diameter:—Set 7854 on C to 10 upon D, and against any diameter on D is the number of superficial inches, feet, &c., on C.

V. Having circumference given to find area, or area to find circumference:—Set ·0795 upon C to 10 on D, then opposite any circumference upon D is the area on C, in whatever the dimensions are set.

TRIANGLES AND POLYGONS.

To find the area of an equilateral triangle, and regular polygons with from 5 to 12 sides; to ascertain length of perpendicular from centre; and to find length of side of the largest of any shaped polygon that can be inscribed in a given circle:—

No. of Sides.	Name of Polygon.	Gauge Point for Area.	Gauge Point Perpendicular.	Size of side of Polygon in Circle.
3	Triangle	·433	·288	1·4
4	Tetragon	1·	·5	1·7
5	Pentagon	1·72	·688	2·06
6	Hexagon	2·598	·866	2·4
7	Heptagon	3·633	1·038	2·77
8	Octagon	4·828	1·2	3·2
9	Nonagon	6·181	1·373	3·54
10	Decagon	7·694	1·538	3·9
11	Undecagon	9·365	1·702	4·3
12	Dodecagon	11·196	1·866	4·62

To ascertain the area set gauge point in first column (opposite number of sides) on C to 1 upon D, and against length of one side on D are superficial contents upon C. The second column is to ascertain length of perpendicular from centre to the exterior, which is done by setting the numbers there on B

B 2

to 1 upon A, opposite to length of side on A is length of perpendicular upon B. Or, having a circle given, and wishing to ascertain the size which any polygon will be described in it, set diameter of the circle on B to the given gauge point in the third column upon A, and opposite to 12 on A is length of side on B.

Ex. 1. What will be the area of an equilateral triangle of 9 inches? Set ·433 upon C to 1 on D, and against 9 on D is 35 upon C. Or, to ascertain what the length of the perpendicular will be, set ·288 upon B to 1 on A, against 9 on A is 2·6 inches on B.

Ex. 2. Required area of a hexagon, each side 14 inches? Set 2·598 on C to 1 upon D, opposite 14 on D is 509 inches upon C.

Ex. 3. What is the superficial measure of a 16-inch octagon? Set 4·828 upon C to 1 on D, against 16 upon D is 1236 on C, and the perpendicular will be found to be 19·2 inches.

Ex. 4. What will be the length of side of the largest decagon that can be inscribed in a circle 18 inches in diameter? Set 18 on B to 3·9 upon A, opposite 12 on A is 5⅓ full upon B.

To find the number of inches in length at any given breadth to make a superficial foot:—Set 12 on B to the breadth in inches upon A, and opposite 12 on A are the number of inches upon B which will make a superficial foot. Or, knowing the size of door and width of board to be used, to ascertain how many feet in length will be required. Set width in inches of door on B to width of board, and opposite length in feet of door on A is its length on B of board required.

Ex. 1. At 2½ inches broad, how many in length does it require to get a foot? Set 12 upon B to 2·5 on A, and against 12 on A is 58 bare upon B.

Ex. 2. If the breadth of a board be 8 inches, how many feet will be wanted for a door 6½ feet × 4 feet? Set 48 on B to 8 on A, and against 6½ on A is 39 feet upon B.

ELLIPSES.

To ascertain the circumference of an ellipsis, first find mean proportional between the two diameters, and set that on B to 3·1416 on A, against 1 upon A is the circumference.

To know the area of an ellipsis :—Set length upon B to 12·75 on A, and against width upon A is superficial contents on B.

Ex. In an ellipsis 24 × 20, we get the area by setting 24 on B to 12·75 upon A, against 20 on A is 377 upon B. Or, to get the circumference, mean proportional on B to 3·1416 on A, and opposite to 1 on A is 70, which is the circumference.

PARABOLAS.

To find the area of a parabola :—Set height upon B to 15 on A, opposite width at base upon A is area on B.

Ex. What is the area of a parabola ⌒ ? Set 11 on B to 15 on A, against 8 upon A is 58·6 on B.

MENSURATION OF SOLIDS.

In measuring square timber, &c., the length in feet on the line C is set to 12 upon D, and opposite the mean proportional of the other dimensions in inches upon D will be found the contents on C in solid feet.

If it should be round, the length on C must be set to 13·54 on D, and then opposite the diameter in inches on D will be found the number of solid feet it contains upon C.

If all dimensions be given in inches, and it should be wished to obtain the answer in cubic inches, then set length on C to 1 on D, and against depth upon D is answer as required on C. If unequal-sided, the answer is found on C opposite mean proportional upon D. Or, for answer in cubic feet, set length to 13·125 on D.

Ex. 1. What are the contents of a piece of timber, 29 feet long, 11 × 17 inches? Find mean proportional between 11 and 17, by setting 11 upon C to 11 on D, and opposite 17 on C is 13·75 on D; then set 29 on C to 12 upon D, and against 13·75 on D is 88 feet on C.

Ex. 2. How many cubic feet are there in a piece of timber, 35 feet 14½ × 19 inches? Set 35 on C to 12 on D, and opposite 16½ full (mean proportional) upon D is 66 feet on C.

Ex. 3. If the length of a round piece is 23 feet, mean diameter 18 inches, how many cubic feet does it contain? Set 23 on C to 13·54 upon D, and against 18 on D is 40½ feet upon C.

Ex. 4. How many feet are there in a piece, length 44 feet, mean diameter 27 inches? Set 44 on C to 13·54 upon D, and opposite 27 on D is 175 feet on C.

Ex. 5. How many cubic inches are there in a piece of timber, 80 inches long, 14 × 18? Set 80 on C to 1 upon D, and against 15·85 on D (mean proportional) is 20·160 cubic inches upon C.

Ex. 6. How many cubic feet are there in a piece of timber, 95 inches, 17 × 22? Set 95 on C to 13·125 upon D, and against 19·3 on D is 20·5 feet upon C.

When the girth of a tree is taken, it is usual to allow 1 inch in every 12 for the bark; thus, if it were 60 inches in circumference, the net girth would be 55 inches.

To obtain an answer in cubic yards, after having found a mean proportional between breadth and depth, set length in feet on C to 5·2 upon D, and against the proportional on D is the answer in cubic yards upon C.

Ex. How many cubic yards are there in a cellar 54 feet long, 36 feet wide, and 8 feet deep, and which now requires to be dug? Set 54 on C to 5·2 on D, and against 17 (mean proportional) upon D is 576 cubic yards on C.

To ascertain the number of inches in length at any given girth to make a solid foot, set 12 on C to a quarter of the given girth upon D, and opposite 12 on D will be found the required number of inches on C.

Ex. If the quarter girth is 8½ inches, how many inches in length are required to make a solid foot? Set 12 on C to 8·5 upon D, and opposite 12 on D are 24 upon C.

CYLINDER, GLOBE, CONE, &c.

To discover the number of cubic inches there are in a cylinder, set depth on C to 11·3 upon D, and opposite diameter on D is the number of cubic inches upon C.

If the answer is required in cubic feet, set depth in feet upon C to 135 full on D, and against diameter in inches upon D is answer in feet on C.

Ex. 1. How many cubic inches are there in a cylinder 22 inches deep, 8 in diameter? Set 22 on C to 11·3 upon D, and opposite 8 on D is 1105 upon C.

Ex. 2. How many feet are contained in a cylinder, 9 feet 6 inches deep, 17 in diameter? Set 9·5 on C to 13·5 full upon D, and against 17 on D is 15 cubic feet upon C.

The manner in which to ascertain the solid contents of a globe, knowing either diameter or circumference, is to set diameter on C to 13·75 full, or circumference, to 77 bare upon D, and opposite same number on D is answer on C.

Ex. 1. How many solid inches are there in a globe, the diameter being 20 inches? Set 20 upon C to 13·75 full on D, and against 20 on D are 4185 cubic inches upon C.

Ex. 2. In a globe 5 feet 6 in diameter, how many cubic feet are contained? Set 5·5 on C to 13·75 full upon D, opposite 5·5 on D is 87 feet on C.

Ex. 3. What will be the number of cubic inches in a globe, 100 inches in circumference? Set 100 upon C to 77 bare on D, and against 100 on D is 17000 cubic inches on C.

Ex. 4. How many cubic feet are there in a globe, the circumference of which is 27 feet? Set 27 on C to 77 bare upon D, opposite 27 on D is 337 feet on C.

For the contents of a cone set one-third of its

perpendicular height on C to 11·3 on D, and against diameter of base upon D are the cubic contents on C.

Ex. What are the contents of a cone 15 inches high, and diameter of base 15 inches? Set 5 (the third of 15) on C to 11·3 upon D, and opposite to 15 on D is 883 cubic inches on C.

For a pyramid, multiply the area of the base by one-third of its perpendicular height.

TO ASCERTAIN THE SOLIDITY, &c., OF ANY REGULAR BODY.

In the first column is given the gauge point to which on A 1 upon B must be set, and opposite the diameter of the sphere on B is given the length of side of the required shape, that may be inscribed in the sphere. The second column has gauge points to be used as the previous one, and opposite the cube of length of its side on B will be found on A its cubic contents. Or, knowing the diameter of a globe, the length of side of any of them equal to the globe may be found :—After setting 1 on B to the given number in the third column on A, then upon the same line will be found the length of side, opposite to the diameter of the globe upon B.

4	Tetrahedron	·8165	·11785	1·6441
6	Hexahedron	·5773	1·	·806
8	Octahedron	·7071	·4714	1·0357
12	Dodecahedron	·5257	7·6631	·6215
20	Icosahedron	·3568	2·1817	·4668

Ex. 1. If I have a globe 15 inches in diameter, what is the length of side of the largest hexahedron that can be cut out of it? Set 1 upon B to ·5773 on A, then opposite 15 upon B is 8·66 on A. For a dodecahedron in same sized globe, set 1 on B to ·5257 upon A, against 15 on B is 7·88 on A.

Ex. 2. What are the cubic contents of a tetrahedron, each side 14 inches in length? Set 1 upon B to ·11785 on A, against 2744 (the cube of 14) on B is 323 cubic inches upon A. For an octahedron, 14 inches, set 1 upon B to ·4714 upon A, and opposite 2744 on B is 1293 cubic inches on A.

Ex. 3. What will be the length of the side of a dodecahedron, equal to a globe 26 inches in diameter? Set 1 on B to 6215 upon A, and against 26 upon B is 16·16 on A. For the side of an icosahedron, equal to same globe, set 1 on B to 4·088 upon A, and opposite to 26 upon B is 10·65 inches on A.

SHAFTS AND PRISMS.

No. of Sides.	Gauge Points.
3	23
5	58
6	385
7	274
8	207
9	161
10	13
11	1063
12	833

To find the solid contents of shafts or prisms polygonally sided, set square of breadth of one of the sides on B to given gauge point upon A, and opposite length of prism on A are the cubic contents on B.

Ex. 1. What are the solid contents of a triangular prism, height 24 inches, breadth of each side 12 inches? Set 144 upon B to 23 on A, against 24 on A is 1,500 cubic inches upon B.

Ex. 2. How many cubic inches are there in a 5-sided body, in length 12 inches, and each side 4 inches? Set 16 on B to 58 upon A, and opposite 12 on A we find 33 on B.

Ex. 3. What are the contents in a shaft with 11 sides, each side 7 inches, and 18 inches in length ? The square of 7 being 49, set that on B to 1063 upon A, and then against 18 on A is 8275 cubic inches upon B.

CYLINDRICAL RINGS.

To ascertain the superficial measurement of circular rings, add width of ring to inner diameter, set that on B to 32 on A, against width upon A is answer on B.

Ex. What are the superficial contents of a ring $2\frac{1}{4}$ inches wide and 6 inches diameter ? Add $2\frac{1}{4}$ to 6, then set $8\frac{1}{4}$ on B to 32 upon A, against $2\frac{1}{4}$ on A is 66·75 upon B.

For solidity, multiply the superficial contents by depth of ring in same dimensions.

CASK GAUGING,

is performed by setting the length upon C to 18·79 on D, then opposite to the mean diameter on D are contents in gallons upon C.

Ex. How many gallons are contained in a cask 28 inches in length, bung diameter 22 inches, head 18 inches ? Set 28 on C to 18·79 upon D. Then against 20 on D are 31·35 gallons on C.

MALT GAUGING.

The usual manner of doing this with the slide rule is first to ascertain the number of bushels that could be laid on the floor at 1 inch deep, and multiply that by the number of inches at which it is

c

laying in depth. To do this, the gauge points for square measure are 2218.

Ex. 1. How many bushels are contained in a cistern or floor 72 inches long, 48 inches wide, and 1 inch deep? Set 72 upon B to 2218 on A, and opposite 48 on A are 1·55 bushels on B.

Ex. 2. If a floor is covered with malt at a depth of 15 inches, and is 39 inches long and 27 inches wide, of how many bushels will it consist? Set 39 on B to 2218 upon A, and against 27 on A is ·475 bare upon B; by then setting that number on B to 1 upon A, we find against 15 on A are 7·12 bushels upon B, and opposite any depth in inches are the number of bushels it will contain.

Another way of doing this, and quite as correctly, is, first, to find a mean proportional (see page 12) between length and width, then set depth on C to 47 upon D for square or unequal-sided vessels, and to 53 full for circular vessels; and opposite mean proportion for square, and diameter for round, on D will be the contents in bushels upon C.

Ex. 1. How many bushels are contained in a cistern 46 feet long, 32 wide, and 18 deep? Find mean proportion between 46 and 32, which is 38·25, then set 18 on C to 47 upon D; against 38·25 on D are 11·9 bushels.

Ex. 2. How many bushels will a cistern hold, diameter 66 inches, and depth 42? Set 42 on C to 53 full upon D; against 66 on D is 64·7 bushels on C. Or, for answer in gallons, set depth of square cisterns to 16·65, for round to 18·8 bare.

STEAM ENGINES.

To ascertain the power of steam engines according to the usual estimate, set 5 on C to 13 bare upon D, or according to Watt, to 11·2 on D; and opposite any diameter of a steam cylinder on the line D, is the number of horses' power on C.

METAL WEIGHING, &c.

The weighing of any body or substance is performed in the same manner as measuring, only the answer will be in cwts., lbs., &c., instead of cubic feet, bushels, gallons, &c.

In the first column of the table given below, is the specific gravity of each substance in ounces, in comparison with water, considering that as 1; and in the second, the actual weight of a cubic foot in pounds avoirdupois. The third column is the number of cubic inches wanted in each given substance to make 1 pound; and the fourth consists of gauge points to which on D to set the diameter of a globe upon C. The fifth is for a bar of metal unequally sided, (having found a mean proportional,) set the length in inches on C to given number on D; then against mean number upon D is weight on C; if the metal be square, use it in the same way as that just mentioned. The sixth and seventh columns are for round bars, the former for length in feet, the last in inches; setting the length either in feet or inches on C to the given gauge point on D, and opposite the diameter upon D is weight on C. Or, if wishing to weigh metal, stone, &c., if it is neither globular, cylindrical, or a kind of bar, first ascertain the number of cubic inches, and divide that by the number of inches in that substance to make 1 lb.

	Specific gravity.	Weight, in lbs.	No. of inches in a pound.	Gauge points for globes.	Square or unequal sided bars.	Round bars.	
						Length, in feet.	Length, in in.
Platinum, purified...	19·5	1218·75	1·4178	16·5bare	11·85	12·37	13·5
,, hammered	20·34	1283·75	1·346	16 full	11·55	12	13·17
,, drawn into wire	22·07	1379·475	1·2526	15·4	11·2	11·55	12·7
Gold, pure and cast	19·26	1203·75	1·435	16·6	12	12·45	13·63
,, hammered ...	19·36	1210	1·4281	16·5	12 bare	12·37	13·5
Mercury	13·57	848·125	2·0374	19·5	14·15	14·6	16
Lead, cast	11·35	709·375	2·436	21·5	15·6	16·11	17·65
Silver, pure and cast	10·47	654·375	2·64	22·4	16·25	16·86	18·5
,, hammered ...	10·51	656·875	2·63	22·5	16·25	16 86	18·5
Bismuth, cast	9·82	613·1875	2·818	23·2	16·75	17·4	19
Copper, cast	8·79	549·375	3·145	24·5	17·75	18·3	20
,, cast wire	8 89	555·625	3·11	24·4	17·7	18·3	20
Brass, cast	8·40	525	3·991	25	18·15	18·75	20·5
,, wire	8·54	533·75	3·287	24·8	18	18·6	20·3
Cobalt & nickel, cast	7·81	488·125	3·54	26	18·5	19·5	21·35
Iron, cast	7·21	450·625	3·835	27	19·6	20·25	22·12
,, malleable	7·79	486·875	3·549	26	18 85	19·5	21·4
Steel, soft	7·83	489·375	3·531	26	18·8	19·5	21·4
,, hammered ...	7·84	490	3·526	26 bare	18·7	19·4	21·3
Tin, cast...............	7·3	456·25	3·787	26·75	19·5	20	21·9
Zinc, cast	7·2	450	3·837	27	19·5	20·2	22
Antimony, cast	4·95	309·375	5·6	32·7	7·5	24·5	26·8
Molybdenum.........	4·74	296·25	5·833	33·3	7·65	25	27·35
Sulphate of barytes.	4·43	276·875	0·25	34·5	7·9	26	28·5
Zircon of Ceylon ...	4·41	275·625	6·27	34·5	8	26	28·5

STONES, EARTHS, &c.

Oriental ruby	4·28	267·5	6·46
Brazilian ditto	3·53	220·6	7·83
Bohemian garnet	4·19	261·62	6·6
Oriental topaz.................	4·01	250·62	7
Diamond....................	3·5	218·75	8
Crude manganese	3·53	220·625	7·83
Flint glass	2·89	180·625	9·56
Glass of St. Gobin	2·49	155·625	11·1
Fluor spar	3·18	198·75	8·7
Parian marble.................	2·34	146·25	11·8
Peruvian marble...............	2·78	173·75	9·94
Jasper......................	2·7	168·875	10·23
Carbonate of lime	2·71	169·375	10·2
Rock crystal	2·65	165·625	10·4
Flint	2·59	161·875	10·67
Sulphate of lime..............	2·32	145	11·91
,, soda..............	2·2	137·5	12·56
Common salt	2·13	133·137	13
Native sulphur	2·03	126·875	13·6
Nitre	2	125	13·8
Alabaster....................	1·87	117	14·8

Phosphorus	1·77	110·625	15·6
Plumbago	1·86	116·25	15
Alum	1·72	107·5	16
Asphaltum	1.4	87·5	20
Jet	1·24	72·5	23·8
Newcastle coal	1·27	79·4	21·9
Staffordshire do.	1·24	77·5	22·2
Sulphuric acid	1·84	115	15·1
Nitric acid	1·22	76·25	22·66
Muriatic acid	1·19	74·375	23·2

LIQUIDS, OILS, &c.

Ice	·92	57·5	30
Strong alcohol	·82	51·25	33·7
Sulphuric ether	·74	46·25	37·3
Naptha	·71	44·375	39
Sea water	1·08	67·5	25·6
Oil of sassafras	1·09	68·125	25·36
Linseed oil	·84	52·5	32·91
Olive oil	·91	56·875	30·3
White sugar	1·61	100·625	17·17

RESINS, GUMS, &c.

Gum arabic and honey	1·43	89·37	19·34
Pitch	1·15	72	24
Isinglass	1·11	70	24·7
Yellow amber	1·08	67·5	25·6
Hen's eggs, fresh laid	1·09	68·12	25·37
Human blood	1·05	65·62	26·3
Camphor	·99	61·87	27·6
White wax	·97	61	28·3
Tallow	·94	58·75	29·4
Pearl	2·75	171·87	10
Sheep's bone	2·22	138·75	12·5
Ivory	1·92	120	14·4
Ox's horn	1·84	115	15

WOOD.

Lignum vitæ	1·33	83·4	20·7
Ebony	1·18	75·75	23·4
Mahogany	1·06	66·5	26
Dry oak	·93	58·2	29·7
Beech	·85	53·2	32·5
Ash	·84	52·9	32·7
Elm .... from	·80	50	34·5
to	·60	37·5	46

c 2

Fir .... from	·57	35·6	50
to	·50	31	55·7
Poplar	·38	24	72
Cork	·24	15	115.2

GASES.

Chlorine	·00303	·19
Carbonic acid gas	·00174	·1087
Oxygen gas	·09132	5·7
Atmospheric air	·00121	·075
Azote	·00117	·073
Hydrogen gas	·00008	·005

Ex. 1. What is the weight of a globe 9 inches in diameter, of pure gold, pure silver, and cast copper? Set 9 on C to 16·6 upon D; and opposite 9 on D is 266 pounds. For pure silver, set 9 on C to 22·4 upon D, and opposite 9 on D is 144 pounds. For cast copper, set 9 to 24·5; and against 9 on D is 121·37 pounds.

Ex. 2. How much will a bar of cast lead, malleable iron, and cast zinc weigh, if it is 7 feet long, 3 × 1½? For cast lead, set 84 on C to 15·6 upon D; against mean proportional 2·125 on D is 155 pounds on C. Malleable iron, 84 to 18·85; opposite 2·125 on D is 106·5 pounds on C. Cast zinc, 84 to 19·5 against 21¼ on D is 98⅓ pounds on C.

Ex. 3. What will be the weight of a round bar of the two following metals, cast iron and bismuth, 8½ feet long and 1¼ inches in diameter? For cast iron set 8·5 feet on C to 20·25 upon D; opposite 1·5 on D is 46·75 pounds on C. Bismuth, 8·5 to 17·4; against 1·5 on D is 63·6 pounds upon C.

Or, taking that as 102 inches, for cast iron, set that number on C to 22·12, and against 1·5 on D is 46·75; while, for bismuth, setting 102 to 19, we have on C opposite to 1·5 on D 63·6 pounds.

GAUGING ANY SHAPED VESSEL.

Wishing for answer in gallons for a square vessel, set depth in inches on C to 16·68 on D; against mean proportional upon D is number of gallons on C. For a globular vessel, set diameter on C to 23 on D, opposite diameter on D is answer upon C.

For a cylinder, set depth on C to 18·79 on D, and against diameter on D is answer; or for an ellipsis, the longest diameter on B to 353 upon A, answer is found on B against other diameter on A. In a triangular prism, superficial contents on B to 277·274 on A, opposite depth on A is the number of gallons upon B. In either rhombus ☐ or rhomboids ☐ set length of side on B to 277·273 upon A, and opposite perpendicular from one to another on A are its contents in gallons. For answer in bushels, for square vessels, set to 15 bare on D; for a globular vessel, diameter to 20·6 on D; for a cylinder, depth to 16·8; ellipsis, longest diameter upon A to 2824 on B; triangular prism, superficial contents on B to 2218 upon A; rhombus ☐ or rhomboids ☐ length of the side on B to 2218 full upon A, and against perpendicular between two lines on A are its contents in bushels.

Ex. 1. How many gallons will a cistern 23 inches square and 15 inches deep contain? Set 15 on C to 16·68 on D, against 23 upon D is 28·6 gallons on C.

Ex. 2. In a globe 18 inches in diameter, how many gallons will there be? Set 18 on C to 23 upon D, and against 18 on D are 11 upon C.

Ex. 3. How many gallons have we in a cylinder 18 inches deep and 9 in diameter ? Set 18 on C to 18·79 upon D, and against 9 on D is 4·13 gallons on C.

Ex. 4. In an elliptic cistern 30 × 24 and 15 inches deep, how many gallons are there ? Set 30 upon B to 353 on A, against 24 on A is 20 full upon B ; then by multiplying that number by 15 (the depth of that cistern) we see it will hold 30¼ gallons.

Ex. 5. What is the number of gallons a triangular prism 24½ inches in height and each side 12 inches in length will contain ? After having ascertained area of the base (which is 62·35) set that on B to 277 full upon A, and against its height 24½ on A is 5½ gallons upon B. If the answer for either of these examples be required in bushels, you have only to set to the other gauge point which is given.

Ex. 6. What is the area in gallons of a rhombus, length of one side 40 inches, and perpendicular 37 inches ? Set 40 upon B to 277 on A, and against 37 on A is 5·337 gallons upon B.

FALLING BODIES.

The velocity acquired by heavy bodies falling near the surface of the earth is 16$\frac{1}{12}$ feet in the first second ; and as 16$\frac{1}{12}$ feet are to the square of one second, or 1, so is the given distance to the square of the seconds required.

Ex. If a stone is let fall into a pit, and should find the bottom at the end of the 8th second, what is the depth of the pit ? Set 16$\frac{1}{12}$ upon C to 1 on D, and against 8 upon D is 1030 feet, the answer on C. The slide being thus set is a table of seconds and feet.

As	2	64·3	are
against	4	257	these
these	6	580	feet
seconds	8	1030	upon
upon D,	10	1609	C.

PENDULUMS.

A pendulum 39·2 inches long in this climate makes just 60 vibrations in one minute of time, and we have found by experience that their lengths are to one another as the square of the number of their vibrations made in the same space of time.

Ex. 1. What will be the length of a pendulum to beat half-seconds, or to make 120 vibrations in a minute? Invert the slide and set 39·2 on B to 60 upon D, and against 120 on D are 9·8 inches on B. As the slide now stands, the lines B and D are a table of inches and vibrations; for opposite any length in inches upon B, you have the number of vibrations on D.

Against 157		30	these
88·5		40	
inches 56·5	are	50	vibrations
39·2		60	
upon B, 28·8		70	upon D.

Ex. 2. If the extreme end of the minute hand of St. Paul's clock should move forward at the rate of 30 inches in 5 minutes, what will be the circumference of that part of the dial plate, and length of the minute hand? Set 5 minutes upon B to 30 inches on A, and opposite 60 minutes on B (as that is one revolution of the hand) stands 360 inches, the circumference of the dial, upon A; then set 1 upon B to 3·14 on A, and opposite 360 on A are

114·58 inches, the diameter of the dial plate, the half of which is the length of the minute hand, about 57·29 inches.

Ex. 3. If a man sets out from Bolton to London, and walks at the rate of 3 miles an hour, and another man starts from London at the same time, going 4 miles an hour, at what distance from each place will they meet, the entire distance being 193 miles? Add 3 to 4, then set that number, viz. 7, on B to the distance 193 upon A, and against 3 on B are 88 miles upon A (the distance from Bolton), and opposite 4 on B are 110 miles upon A, (the distance from London.)

MACHINERY.

I. Knowing pitch of tooth and diameter of wheel, to ascertain number of cogs or teeth :—Set pitch of tooth upon B to 3·14 on A, and against the diameter upon B is the number of cogs on A.

Ex. In a wheel 50 inches in diameter at the pitch line, how many teeth, in pitch exactly $1\frac{1}{2}$ inches, shall we have? Set $1\frac{1}{2}$ on B to 3·14 on A, and opposite 50 upon B is 104 on A.

II. The diameter at pitch line and number of teeth being given, to ascertain pitch of tooth :—Set diameter on B to number of teeth upon A, and the pitch of the tooth will be found on B opposite to the gauge point 3·14 upon A.

Ex. What will be the pitch of the tooth on a wheel 65 inches in diameter which has 136 teeth? Set 65 upon B to 136 on A, and against 3·14 on A is $1\frac{1}{2}$ inch upon B.

III. To find the diameter, having pitch and number of teeth given :—Set the pitch of the tooth upon B to 3·14 on A, and opposite number of teeth upon A is diameter of wheel on B.

Ex.—What is the diameter of a wheel having 48 teeth of a 2-inch pitch ? Set 2 upon B to 3·14 on A, and against 48 on A is 30¼ inches, the diameter, upon B.

IV. Having the revolutions of two wheels given, with the diameter of one of them, to find the diameter of the other :—Set number of revolutions the wheel makes in 1 minute on C to inches it is in diameter upon A, and against number of revolutions the small one makes in the same time on C is its diameter upon A.

Ex. If a wheel 150 inches in diameter makes 5 revolutions in a minute, what will be the diameter of another working in it, that is to make 68 revolutions in the same time ? Invert the slide, and set 5 upon C to 150 on A, and against 68 upon C is the diameter of the small wheel, viz., 11 inches.

Unwin, Gresham Steam Press, 31, Bucklersbury, London.